young CHANGEMAKERS
COMPASSIONATE KIDS

Written By
STACY C. BAUER

Illustrated By
EMANUELA NTAMACK

This book is dedicated to Grace, Madison, Rosie, Arabella, Callie, Matine, Oliver, Kennedi, Alex, Joris, Pavel and Katie. Keep shining brightly for all the world to see. Keep changing the world.

Compassionate Kids
Young Change Makers
Published by Hop Off the Press, LLC
www.stacycbauer.com

Minneapolis, MN

Book design by Travis D. Peterson.

Library of Congress Control Number: 2021919575
Bauer, Stacy C. Author
Ntamack, Emanuela Illustrator
Compassionate Kids

ISBN: 978-1-7373890-2-6

JUVENILE NONFICTION

Printed in the United States.

All inquiries of this book can be sent to the author.
For more information, please visit **www.stacycbauer.com**

MEET THE CHANGE MAKERS!

INSPIRATIONAL ICONS
Chasing their dreams and
encouraging others to do the same!

Grace 4

Madison 10

Rosie 19

Callie 28

Arabella 34

HELPING HANDS
Delivering support to those in need.

Matine 7

Oliver 16

Kennedi 22

Alex 31

ANIMAL AMBASSADORS
Helping and advocating for animals.

Joris 13

Pavel 25

CONSERVATION CREW
Saving the planet.

Katie 37

GRACE

Maryland, USA

WELCOME to CAMP HAPPY

"HAPPINESS SHOULDN'T HAVE TO WAIT."

Meet Grace Callwood, the founder of the We Cancerve Movement. We Cancerve's motto is that happiness shouldn't have to wait. They focus on quick solutions that empower kids to help other kids in need—from homeless or sick children to those in foster care.

Grace has been helping others since she was two years old, when she asked her parents to donate a red wagon to a local hospital for the kids to ride around in. For her third and fourth birthdays, she asked for donations instead of gifts, and at age four, she collected food and donated it to the Hurricane Katrina relief fund.

When Grace was seven, she was diagnosed with a type of cancer called **Non-Hodgkin's Lymphoma**. Grace had to have chemotherapy and the medicines made her gain weight, so she donated her brand-new school clothes to two little girls who had lost

NON-HODGKIN'S LYMPHOMA is a cancer that starts in the lymphatic system when the body produces too many lymphocytes, a type of white blood cell.

FOSTER CARE provides kids a safe and caring place to live until their families can take care of them again.

everything in a fire. The girls' happy reactions inspired her to do more acts of kindness for others–especially children.

Grace realized that, even while fighting cancer, she could help other kids in sad situations. So, with the help of her parents, seven-year-old Grace started her own nonprofit: We Cancerve.

Grace is passionate about helping homeless or sick children and children in **foster care**. When she was ten years old, Grace created Camp Happy, a free summer camp for homeless children. A few years later, her nonprofit helped Camp Happy grow to include a foster care group home and introduced a virtual camp that has reached children throughout America and as far away as India! We Cancerve also opened La Magnifique Boutique, a free shop that provides shoes,

clothing, and jewelry to teen girls living in foster care. The group helps families of sick children and opens up children's libraries. She has been

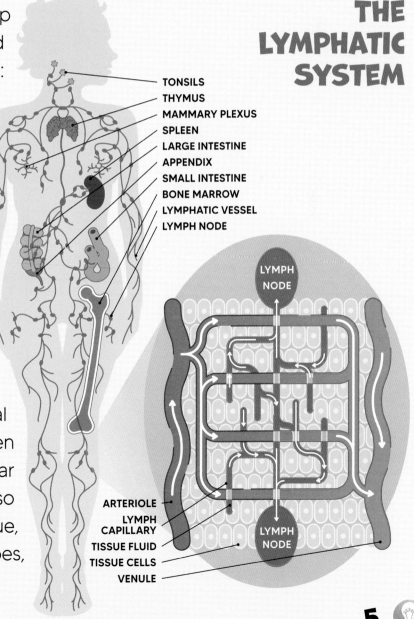

THE LYMPHATIC SYSTEM

TONSILS
THYMUS
MAMMARY PLEXUS
SPLEEN
LARGE INTESTINE
APPENDIX
SMALL INTESTINE
BONE MARROW
LYMPHATIC VESSEL
LYMPH NODE

LYMPH NODE

LYMPH NODE

ARTERIOLE
LYMPH CAPILLARY
TISSUE FLUID
TISSUE CELLS
VENULE

awarded thousands of dollars in national and global prizes for her service work, and she's raised more than $300,000 in donations.

After about three years of chemo-therapy, Grace was cancer-free. In the future, she hopes to get involved in government, so that she can help the people who need it the most.

GRACE'S FUN FACTS:

- **Grace is Caribbean-American.**
- **She loves music and plays the trumpet and the French horn.**
- **Her favorite things to bake are banana bread and brownies.**

BECOME A young CHANGEMAKERS™ INSPIRATIONAL ICON!

- **Visit Grace's website to learn more about her movement and see how you can help:** www.wecancerve.org

- **What do you like to do? Find a nonprofit near you that needs help and get involved!**

GRACE'S ADVICE FOR YOU:
Find your passion, gather support, and stay committed to making a difference.

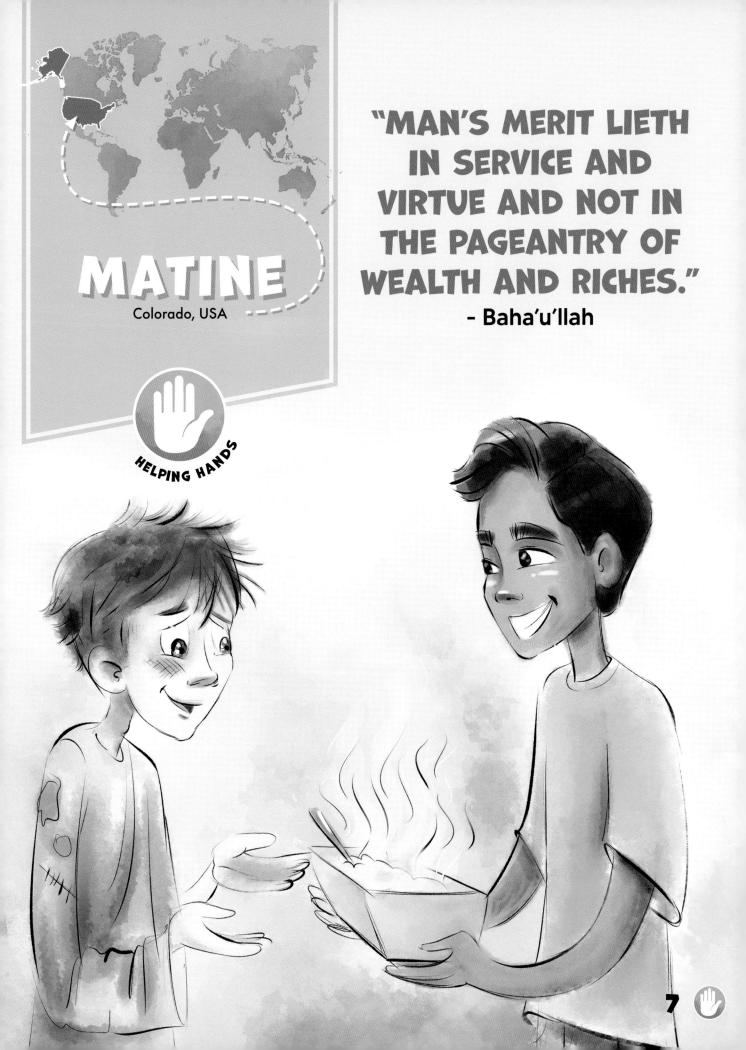

MATINE

Colorado, USA

HELPING HANDS

"MAN'S MERIT LIETH IN SERVICE AND VIRTUE AND NOT IN THE PAGEANTRY OF WEALTH AND RICHES."

- Baha'u'llah

MATINE'S FUN FACTS:

- **Matine loves hiking.**
- **He enjoys traveling.**
- **He loves trying out new foods.**

Have you ever felt a calling to make a difference in your community? When Matine Khalighi was in eighth grade, he knew he wanted to help those less fortunate than himself. After taking a class about how kids can get involved in their communities, Matine decided to take action. He spent many hours doing **storefront fundraising** and raised over $1,000 for a local foster care center. While giving the money to the foster care center felt great, for Matine the best part was meeting the kids who benefitted from his effort.

Driven by the joy he found in helping others, Matine was inspired to keep doing more. He was surprised as he traveled around his own neighborhood to see how many people were struggling with homelessness. Even more surprising was the lack of resources available to help them.

Determined to change that, Matine co-founded Helping the Homeless Colorado (HTHC), a teen-run nonprofit organization. Four years later, with the help of more than thirty student leaders, Helping the Homeless Colorado raised over $140,000 and distributed over 50,000 basic necessities to people out on the streets!

Matine then noticed that many of the homeless people his nonprofit was providing supplies for were young students, like himself. In fact, over 1.5 million students have experienced homelessness in the United States over the past three years. Inspired to do something even more to help out those young people, HTHC turned into **EEqual**–which stands for Education Equality–a youth-led nonprofit supporting students living in poverty. Since EEqual's launch, Matine and his team have already raised over

When Matine did **STOREFRONT FUNDRAISING**, he asked local store owners if he could set up a table outside of their business. He then talked to people about his cause as they entered and left the store.

A **GRANT** is money given by the government or a business that doesn't have to be repaid.

$13,000 and expanded their youth-led team to over 35 people. EEqual also created a scholarship program to help some homeless students go to college. One of their scholars got a full scholarship to the University of Denver, while another is now a vet tech, working full-time!

Matine and his team do everything themselves, from organizing 5K races and benefit parties to applying for **grants** to raise funds for their program, but it wasn't always easy. In the beginning, Matine and his team struggled to get support because of their ages. They were turned down for grants, businesses ignored their pitches, and adults dismissed their mission. They didn't let that stop them, though. Through hard work and perseverance, they found people who supported them and their goal of helping others!

BECOME A

young CHANGEMAKERS™ HELPING HAND!

- **Visit www.eequal.org to find out more about Matine's cause!**

- **Find out how to help the homeless in your area. Can you volunteer at a soup kitchen or a food bank?**

MATINE'S ADVICE FOR YOU:
In the beginning, my biggest fear was centered around what was going to happen when I made the ask. I remember always being nervous when presenting at pitch contests, talking to new donors, or asking people to support EEqual. Then I started to take to heart the idea that the worst thing that anyone can say is 'no' and you have to approach someone new!

Matine

9

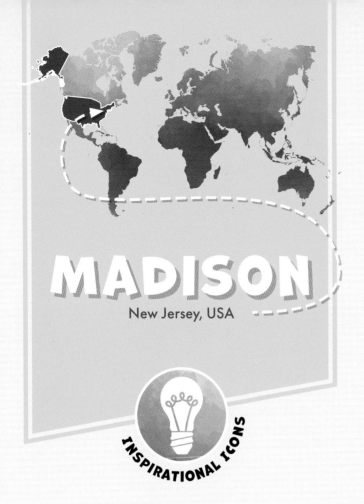

MADISON

New Jersey, USA

INSPIRATIONAL ICONS

"WE ARE ALL DIFFERENT AND THAT IS OKAY."

Did you know that only about 30 percent of children's books are written about racially diverse characters or subjects? Madison Franklin wants to change that. She wants families and teachers to have more diverse libraries. Why? Because reading books about people who are different from us can teach us about different cultures. During the COVID-19 pandemic, the public libraries were closed. Madison wanted kids to have access to important books about diversity and inclusion, so she decided to open her own library!

The first thing Madison did was ask for help. Her mom posted her idea on social media and people started donating books. Her community has supported Madison's mission in amazing and important ways. Madison's city police department and mayor held a ribbon-cutting event when she opened her library, complete with a DJ and an ice cream truck. Police officers and teachers even showed up to read books. Since then, Madison has organized several other community events, such as author readings, that have made it possible for her to see family and friends in a safe way during the pandemic.

Madison has given away thousands of books to children and teachers in need. She has sent books to places as far away as Africa and Peru. She has used her library as a tool to get people working together to help others.

Madison's favorite part of her mission is seeing how happy people are to get books to read. It's important to her that everyone knows it is okay, great even, to be different.

MADISON'S MAGICAL LIBRARY

young CHANGEMAKERS™
INSPIRATIONAL ICON!

- Collect your books that you don't read anymore and donate them.

- Buy some brand new books to donate.

- Visit www.facebook.com/groups/3219117964773410 to find out more about Madison's library!

MADISON'S ADVICE FOR YOU:

If you want to make a difference, just do it!

MADISON'S FUN FACTS:

- Madison has two dogs and a bunny.

- She enjoys doing science experiments and arts and crafts.

- Madison likes to eat her dessert before dinner.

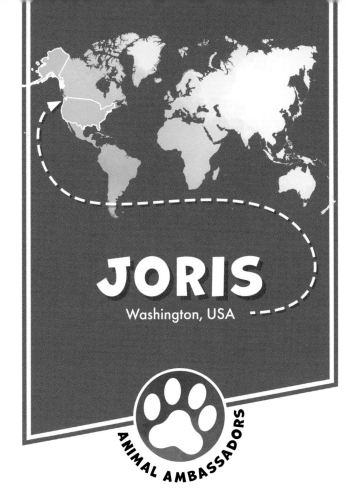

JORIS
Washington, USA

ANIMAL AMBASSADORS

"WHEN WE PROTECT CHEETAHS, THE WHOLE ECOSYSTEM BENEFITS!"

Do you have a favorite animal? Which one is it? Joris Hutchison loves cheetahs. When he was six years old, he read a book about cheetahs and learned that they might go extinct in his lifetime. He was inspired to help change that.

Joris asked his mother for advice on how to help and she began researching wildlife sanctuaries and organizations in Africa. That's when she found **N/a'an ku sê Wildlife Sanctuary**, an organization in Namibia that Joris and his family still work with today!

Joris began small, just asking family and friends to donate to the cause. But he has tried many different things since then. Joris and his mother have made lemonade stands, hosted T-shirt fundraisers and garage sales, asked for donations instead of birthday gifts, and more. Joris is always brainstorming creative ways to raise funds for the sanctuary. In just over eight years, he has raised over $36,000!

Since the biggest threat to cheetahs is struggles with humans, the money Joris has raised goes mainly toward **GPS** collars for cheetahs that have been captured on private land. Often, farmers want to shoot cheetahs because they think the big cats will kill and eat their livestock. When a farmer traps a cheetah in a **capture cage**, they call the sanctuary, who sends out a team to collar the cheetah. They then work with the farmer to monitor the movements of the cheetah to see if it has been causing an issue. The goal is to prevent livestock losses, and in the case of losses, to know if it is a cheetah that is responsible. Getting farmers on board with this plan is essential to saving cheetahs. Each farm is many square miles in size, which means if a farmer can be convinced to live peacefully

SAVE CHEETAHS
SAVE THE WORLD
kids4cheetahs

JORIS' FUN FACTS:

- **Joris is bilingual in English and Dutch, and is a dual citizen of the US and the Netherlands.**

- **He loves international football (soccer).**

- **He can name all 196 countries in 8 minutes and 55 seconds.**

- **He once flew in a helicopter with a wildlife vet while she darted a rhino.**

N/A'AN KU SÊ WILDLIFE SANCTUARY provides a safe haven and second chance for injured, orphaned, and conflict animals. Whenever possible, their aim is to release animals back into the wild.

GPS stands for Global Positioning System. The GPS collars allow the cheetah to be tracked.

A **CAPTURE CAGE** is a cage that traps an animal without hurting it.

with carnivores instead of shooting them, their land can become another important safe zone for the animals.

Every year, Joris and his mother travel to Namibia to volunteer at the sanctuary. They do things like researching, sorting through camera trap photos, feeding/preparing food for captive animals that are too used to humans to be released again, and tracking carnivores. Joris hopes to pursue a career in wildlife conservation in the future. He believes the situation is getting better for cheetahs, but we all need to work together to ensure they are around in the future.

BECOME A

- **Donate to Joris's cause. Visit kids4cheetahs.com to find out more!**

- **Learn more about how you can help your favorite animal!**

- **Visit naankuse.com/ conservation/wildlife- sanctuary to learn more about the N/a'an ku sê Wildlife Sanctuary.**

JORIS' ADVICE FOR YOU:

It doesn't matter what you're doing, it always starts by taking the first step. Just try something, because doing something is better than doing nothing!

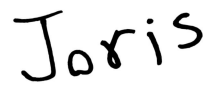

OLIVER

Connecticut, USA

HELPING HANDS

"IT'S IMPORTANT TO ME THAT EVERY KID HAS A WARM AND COZY NIGHT. EVERYONE DESERVES TO FEEL WARM AND SNUGGLY WHEN FALLING ASLEEP."

When Oliver Koenig-Paquin was in preschool, his teacher partnered with **Scholastic** to do a pajama drive. In exchange for donating a pair of pajamas, each child would earn a free book. At first, Oliver was just excited about the book! But when he learned that there are some kids who don't have warm, cozy pajamas to wear to bed at night, he wanted to help! He asked both of his moms to buy 100 pairs of pajamas to donate to the school pajama drive. Instead of buying 100 pairs, Oliver's parents encouraged him to ask family and friends to donate. Oliver did, and during his first year collecting, he was able to donate 122 pairs of pajamas!

When Oliver went to kindergarten, he wanted to keep collecting and donating pajamas. His new school wasn't doing a pajama drive, so his parents contacted Scholastic and were able to make sure every child who received a pair of pajamas from Oliver would also receive a free book from Scholastic! That second year, Oliver collected 223 pairs of pajamas. In first grade, he collected 577 pairs. In second grade, he collected 1,446 pairs. And in third grade, he collected 3,460 pairs!

OLIVER'S FUN FACTS:

- Oliver loves hunting for shark teeth.
- He enjoys playing sports.
- He likes fishing and playing Minecraft.

SCHOLASTIC is the world's largest publisher and distributor of children's books.

Every year, Oliver works with the National Pajama Program Connecticut Chapter to identify the organizations in Connecticut that need new pajamas. Oliver also likes the fact that every child gets a new book, since one of his favorite parts of his bedtime routine is his parents reading to him.

Oliver now has a Facebook page called Oliver's Pajama Project. He and his parents hang flyers, meet new people, fold and organize pajamas, book television interviews, and collect and drop off the pajamas. Oliver also meets with local businesses who want to see how they can help. Some businesses offer to be the collection spot for pajamas, some give prizes and free food to people who donate pajamas, some let Oliver hang flyers, and several businesses collect pajamas for Oliver's mission! For a couple of months every winter, there are so many pajamas at Oliver's house that there isn't anywhere to sit! Luckily, his grandma comes over and helps sort the pajamas into boxes by size. Last year, Oliver had so many boxes of pajamas to donate that he almost couldn't keep up!

In the past five years he has donated over 5,000 pairs! Oliver plans to continue collecting pajamas; his goal for next year is 7,000 pairs!

BECOME A young CHANGEMAKERS™ HELPING HAND!

- **Start your own collection to help people with their basic needs. You could collect and donate food items, clothing, or even soap and toothbrushes.**

- **Learn more about Oliver's Pajama Project here: www.facebook.com/ OliversPajamaProject**

OLIVER'S ADVICE FOR YOU:
No matter how old you are, you can always help others and make a difference in your community. You can accomplish anything you put your mind to.

Oliver

ROSIE

Illinois, USA

INSPIRATIONAL ICONS

"KINDNESS IS THE KEY TO THE WORLD."

At two and a half, Rosie Quinn was diagnosed with Alopecia–a disease that results in baldness. Instead of focusing on fixing her baldness, her parents focused on raising a little girl who loves herself, hair or no hair.

When she was five, Rosie's mother took some of Rosie's paintings and created a head scarf for Rosie to wear. Rosie loved the gift! But having something so unique made her feel sad for other kids who weren't as lucky. So she decided that she wanted to help other kids who looked like her be happy, too.

Rosie asked her mom to quit her full time job so that they could figure out how to donate scarves to the "bald kids." After convincing her mom she was serious, they started their own nonprofit: Coming Up Rosies.

"'Coming Up Roses' is a phrase that means everything is turning out okay. Even though Rosie is sometimes sad about her hair loss, she teaches us with her smile that everything is 'Coming Up Rosies.'"

WWW.COMINGUPROSIES.COM

ROSIE'S FUN FACTS:

- **She loves reading books, especially Harry Potter.**

- **She broke her wrist skateboarding.**

- **She has voted for a bill on the floor of Congress.**

- **Her favorite meal is macaroni and cheese.**

Since 2016, Rosie's nonprofit has donated over 1,500 Smile Kits to hospitals and charity organizations around the world. The Smile Kits come with paint, brushes, and a canvas. Once kids paint their designs on the canvas, they can take a photo and upload it to cominguprosies.com. They can then choose to have a cape, neck scarf, face mask, or head scarf made with that design! Rosie's goal is to help other kids smile and love themselves, no matter what they look like.

Rosie's mission goes beyond just helping kids around the world smile and gain confidence, though. She has also brought awareness to Alopecia. She tries to educate kids on how to be kind to each other, especially to those who look different than they do. Rosie's nonprofit sets a fundraising goal each year and uses the funds raised to donate more Smile Kits to kids who need them.

BECOME A

- **Read more about Rosie's mission and how you can help at:** www.cominguprosies.com

- **Do something TODAY to make someone smile.**

- **Be kind to others who look different than you. If you notice another child being made fun of, stand up for them. Tell the kids to STOP or get an adult. Ask that child to play with you.**

ROSIE'S ADVICE FOR YOU:

Be kind to others and yourself. Being different is what makes the world a better place. If we were the same, life would be very boring.

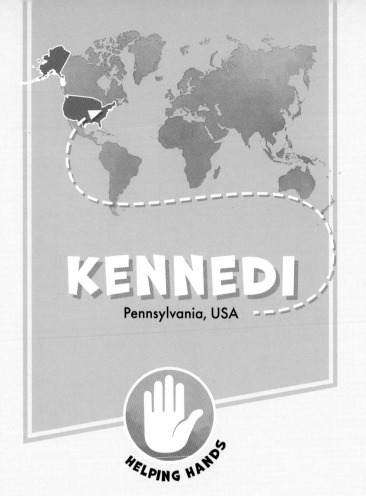

KENNEDI

Pennsylvania, USA

HELPING HANDS

"BELIEVE IN YOURSELF AND ALWAYS BE KIND!"

Is there someone in your life who inspires you to help others? Kennedi Washington's mother is her inspiration. When Kennedi was three, she and her mother began volunteering at the local soup kitchen. They served meals to people who were hungry, and also handed out "blessing bags" filled with water, socks, food, soap, and more.

Since then, Kennedi has tried to live her life in a way that helps others. On her eighth birthday, she asked for donations to the local animal shelter instead of gifts, and has continued that request every year since.

Along with encouraging her to serve others, Kennedi's mother also instilled in her a love of reading. In 2018, Kennedi opened a Little Free Library in front of her house. Her library is full of autographed books donated by authors! She is excited to get books into the hands of kids who need them. Kennedi wants every child to have access to books and to learn to love reading as much as she does.

A ZONING OFFICER decides what can be built and where it can go in a community.

Helping others is not always easy. In order to put up her library, Kennedi had to talk to the **zoning officer** at city hall. Then, after she was approved, the homeowners association told her she had to take it down. She attended several meetings in order to make sure she could continue with this project. She learned the value of determination and not giving up on your dreams!

In the future, Kennedi would like to volunteer at the animal shelter and start her own nonprofit organization.

KENNEDI'S FUN FACTS:

- Kennedi's favorite food is cheese fries.

- She loves visiting Barbados.

- She enjoys shopping.

- Her biggest fear is spiders.

BECOME A

young CHANGEMAKERS™ HELPING HAND!

- **Talk to a grownup about serving meals at a homeless shelter or soup kitchen.**

- **Collect donations for an animal shelter.**

- **Learn more about Kennedi at:** instagram.com/booksthroughmyeyes

KENNEDI'S ADVICE FOR YOU:

If you want to make a difference, believe in yourself, speak up and speak loud! It only takes one person! You can do it!

PAVEL

Arzamas, Russia

ANIMAL AMBASSADORS

25

When Pavel Abramov was seven years old, his beloved cat Barsik died. Saddened by the loss, he started to notice the stray animals wandering the streets of his city. Seeing that they needed help, he decided to do something in Barsik's memory—which he did, in a very creative way. A talented artist, Pavel put his passion to work by starting Kind Paintbrush, a service in which Pavel paints beautiful pictures of people's pets in exchange for donations of food and other supplies to the local animal shelter.

Pavel began Kind Paintbrush by visiting and volunteering at the animal shelter with his mother. His local shelter is the only one in town and currently houses over 100 dogs. Pavel is the youngest volunteer there—but maybe one of the most enthusiastic! He and his mother not only volunteer at the shelter and donate supplies he earns from his

PAVEL'S FUN FACTS:

- Pavel loves to play chess.
- He likes to make and eat pizza.
- He enjoys karate and math.
- He wants to go to art school.

paintings, they also organize events to raise money and to teach kids how to take care of animals.

Kind Paintbrush is now an international movement to help animals in shelters. To date, Pavel has sent about 150 paintings to 15 countries and has around 1,000 more orders waiting for him to fulfill. Thanks to the success of Kind Paintbrush, Pavel has been able to donate more than three tons of food, medicine, household items, and repair materials to the shelter!

An **ARCHITECT** is someone who plans and designs buildings.

Since the only animal shelter in his town is for dogs, Pavel built a shelter for cats with his parents called the Art Pate Creative Cat Studio. His family rescues stray cats from the streets and houses them there. They also vaccinate them and help them find their forever homes. He holds charity events there to help raise money for the animals and teaches children to care for animals through special kindness classes. Pavel dreams of becoming an **architect** and building a large house for animals.

BECOME A young CHANGEMAKERS™ ANIMAL AMBASSADOR!

- **Find an animal shelter near you. Call or visit them. How can you help?**

- **Adopt a stray animal if you can.**

- **Foster some animals who need a safe place to live while they await adoption.**

PAVEL'S ADVICE FOR YOU:

To change the world, you need to start with yourself and ask, "What can I do on my own?" When people see that even a small child is capable of much, they begin to think about themselves. Always believe in a dream, if it is good, then it is destined to come true! Never give up! Failure is just an excuse to set a new, better goal!

CALLIE

Alabama, USA

INSPIRATIONAL ICONS

28

"DREAM BIG. JUST BECAUSE YOU'RE SMALL DOESN'T MEAN YOU CAN'T DO BIG THINGS."

Have you ever written a book? Callie Chapman wrote her first story at age six for a contest at school. It was about a unicorn named Glitter (a stuffed unicorn her brother won for her at a carnival) and her best friend Ellie (Callie's favorite blanket). After the contest ended, her mother brought her story to life with illustrations and made it into a book to give to family and friends. When they got the book from the printer, they decided to try to sell it. Callie then had the idea to donate all of the money they raised to the children's hospital for art supplies. Art makes Callie happy, and she wanted the kids at the hospital to be happy too!

Since then, Callie has written and published three books in her series *Glitter the Unicorn*. Writing makes her happy, and she enjoys creating new adventures. She has sold about 10,000 books so far and donated over $20,000 to local children's hospitals. Her books have even won national awards!

She enjoys visiting schools to speak and inspire young children.

Callie's mission with her book series is to inspire kids to follow their dreams and to give to others. She wants kids to always be kind.

Despite her success, one of Callie's biggest challenges is putting herself "out there". Speaking in front of big groups makes her nervous, but she does it anyway. She once spoke in front of 550 teachers, and has spoken in front of entire schools about her experience!

Callie plans to publish the next two *Glitter the Unicorn* books soon, and hopes to continue inspiring young children by speaking about her experience. She also plans to keep donating art supplies to the children's hospital and to publish books in a new series she has started, *Chandler the Best Unicorn Rider*.

BECOME A **young CHANGEMAKERS™ INSPIRATIONAL ICON!**

CALLIE'S FUN FACTS:

- Callie plays soccer.

- She loves to draw.

- She is in Girl Scouts.

- Callie loves going to camp.

- She loves animals.

- **Check out Callie's books:** www.glittertheunicorn.com

- **Follow her on social media and encourage her with kind words.**

- **Do something kind for the children at a hospital near you!**

CALLIE'S ADVICE FOR YOU:

Dream big! Work hard! If you can imagine it, you can do it.

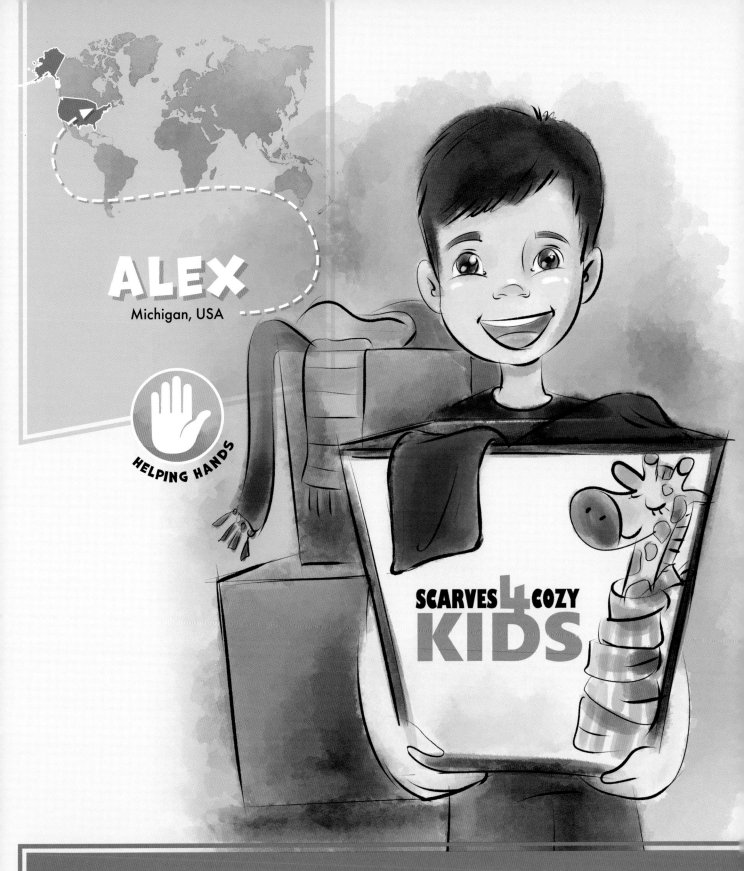

ALEX
Michigan, USA

HELPING HANDS

SCARVES 4 COZY KIDS

"THERE NEEDS TO BE MORE GOOD
PUT OUT INTO THE WORLD."

Have you ever been cold? So cold, that you just couldn't get warm? What did you do? When Alex VanHaren was in fourth grade, he noticed something that changed his life. While playing outside at recess, Alex saw a group of kids standing near the entrance to the school, trying to stay warm. Alex was shocked. None of them had winter clothing. Not only did that make Alex realize how lucky he was that he had warm clothes, but it made him want to help get winter clothing to kids who needed it. When he got home from school, he told his mom he wanted to learn how to knit and why. That very day, they looked up knitting on YouTube and learned how to loom—a faster, easier version of knitting. That year, he made and donated 200 hats, gloves, and scarves to children in need. That's how Alex's Scarves 4 Cozy Kids was born!

Since then, Alex has inspired local nursing home residents and other people to knit with him. Together, they have donated over 8,000 winter items to 45 schools, where kids can take what they need. Alex's Scarves 4 Cozy Kids also does annual and monthly collections for many other organizations.

ALEX'S FUN FACTS:

- **Alex LOVES dogs. He fostered dogs for a rescue when he was younger, and he does yearly collections for local animal shelters.**

- **He plays the snare drum in the high school marching band.**

- **He loves to create things in Minecraft, using cardboard or his 3D pen/printer.**

Many people help Alex with his mission. Delivery drivers drop off the winter supplies at schools. Knitters make winter clothing donations. Donors buy things to give or donate items that they already have. They also supply the charity with yarn. Alex creates the social media posts, counts and takes pictures of donations, and moves and organizes the items.

Alex also loves to help other non-profit organizations raise awareness, collect donation items, and distribute items to people in need. Each month, Alex's organization chooses another nonprofit organization to help. These include saving pop tops for the Ronald McDonald House, eyeglasses for the Lions Club, and collecting and donating food to local food pantries.

For his community service, Alex was awarded the Caring Award. This important award has been given to only 300 other remarkable people who have dedicated their lives to service!

Alex loves seeing the difference his charity makes and wants to help more people in the future.

BECOME A young CHANGEMAKERS™ HELPING HAND!

- **Donate clothing that no longer fits.**

- **Learn to knit or sew and make clothing for others.**

- **Check out Alex's charity to learn more: facebook.com/ scarves4cozykids**

ALEX'S ADVICE FOR YOU:
Start small with what you can do. Every little action causes a ripple effect. There's no action too small to make a positive impact in someone's life.

ARABELLA

Colorado, USA

INSPIRATIONAL ICONS

it's always
CUE
O' CLOCK

"WHEN I GROW UP I WANT TO MAKE IT POSSIBLE FOR PEOPLE TO TELL THE DIFFERENCE BETWEEN SIGN LANGUAGE AND CUED SPEECH."

When Arabella Rose was just five years old, she started creating videos through a YouTube series called "It's Always Cue O'Clock!" in order to teach others about Cued Speech. She is not deaf or hard of hearing, but both of her parents are. They were raised with Cued Speech, instead of sign language, and wanted to be able to communicate well with their hearing daughter, so they began teaching Arabella Cued Speech when she was a newborn. Her dad videoed their experience, and those videos are now used to educate the parents of deaf or hard-of-hearing kids about Cued Speech.

Arabella began creating the videos because she knows there are not many resources about Cued Speech available, and not many people even know what it is. In fact, when they see her and her parents communicating, people think they are using sign language.

The idea of Cued Speech is to make spoken language visual so people can understand different speech sounds even if they look the same on the lips. With Cued Speech, people put together handshapes and hand placements around the mouth. This is called "cueing". The handshapes represent consonants and hand placements represent vowels. These consonants and vowels are **phonemes**. Handshapes and hand placement are put together one at a time to show the individual phonemes and syllables of words.

Through Cued American English, people can see the English language exactly as people speak it. Arabella's mother took three years of German in high school and was able to learn how to speak the language because she could see the German sounds through the Cued Speech system.

In the future, Arabella wants to continue to educate people about Cued Speech.

A **PHONEME** is the smallest unit of a word that has no meaning by itself. For example, "thick" has 3 phonemes: /th/, /i/, /k/.

- Educate yourself about Cued Speech through Cue College (cuecollege.org)

- Watch Arabella's videos: Youtube.com/CueCognatio

- Support the National Cued Speech Association (cuedspeech.org)

ARABELLA'S FUN FACTS:

- Arabella's favorite subject in school is reading.

- She loves watching Biz Kids and Shark Tank.

- She enjoys reading the Boxcar Children, Harry Potter, and Unicorn Academy book series.

- Her favorite sports are gymnastics, soccer, and snowboarding.

- She's trying to learn how to crochet so she can make toy animals for children who are in the hospital.

ARABELLA'S ADVICE FOR YOU:

Follow your dream and don't stop.

arabella

"WE CAN MAKE A DIFFERENCE, ONE VEGETABLE GARDEN AT A TIME."

Do you have a garden? Have you ever grown your own food? When Katie Stagliano was nine years old, she received a cabbage seedling from school. Every day she watered it, fertilized it, and weeded around it. When it was fully grown, it weighed forty pounds–the average cabbage weighs two pounds, so this was truly amazing! Katie decided to donate her cabbage to help feed people who don't have enough food. When she and her parents walked into Tri-County Family Ministries to donate her cabbage, she was surprised by the number of people who were waiting in line for what was probably their only meal that day. The following day, she was invited to help serve her cabbage to 275 people. That experience changed Katie's life. Seeing how many people her one cabbage could feed inspired her to create Katie's Krops.

Katie began with her own garden, donating the produce to Tri-County Family Ministries, but she wanted to do more. When she was in fourth grade, she spoke to her school about her idea. They donated a plot the size of a football field for her to create a garden in order to help those in need. She began hearing from kids around the United States who wanted to help. Nine years ago, she began giving funds to kids to create Katie's Krops gardens in their own communities so that more food could be donated to the hungry. Katie's Krops now has 100 gardens growing across the country and has donated thousands and thousands of pounds of fresh produce to people in need.

The mission of Katie's Krops is to empower kids to start and maintain vegetable gardens of all sizes, and to donate the harvest to help feed people in need. Katie's Krops' "Growers,"–aged 9-16–run gardens in their backyards, school yards, and anywhere they can get permission to grow produce. In total, about 250,000 pounds of produce have been donated since 2008, not just feeding hungry mouths, but also changing the future for thousands of people in the United States.

About ten years ago, one of the soup kitchens Katie had been donating produce to had to close down due to lack of funding. Katie was upset that the people who had been relying on that place for food now had nowhere to go, so she created "Katie's Krops Dinners",

KATIE'S FUN FACTS:

- **Katie's favorite vegetable is snow peas.**

- **She has a puppy named Jax.**

- **Her favorite subject in school was English.**

- **She loves the color blue.**

- **Her favorite food is sushi!**

38

a monthly sit-down meal served at a local church. Each month, 150-200 people receive a meal.

Katie adjusted her organization's offerings to make sure hungry families could still receive food during the COVID-19 pandemic by offering weekly drive-up dinners for her community. In 2020 alone, they served over 18,000 hot, healthy, and free meals to those in need.

In May of 2020, Katie graduated from college with a degree in communications, and has since returned to Katie's Krops full time. She wants to continue to expand Katie's Krops to have gardens in all 50 states and empower even more youth to grow a healthy end to hunger.

"Overall, the goal of Katie's Krops is to end hunger. I know that can be seen as a lofty goal, but working together, we can make a difference, one vegetable garden at a time."–Katie

BECOME A

- **Become a Katie's Krops grower! Find out more at** katieskrops.com

- **Support Katie's mission at** katieskrops.com

- **Grow your own garden and find a way to donate produce in your community.**

KATIE'S ADVICE FOR YOU:

"Follow your heart and find a cause you believe in! It doesn't matter how young or how old you are, or how large or small your efforts are. You can change the world! You never know the ripple effect of one small action."

STACY C. BAUER

A native of Minneapolis, MN, Stacy C. Bauer is a wife, teacher, mother of two and owner of Hop Off the Press—a publisher of quality children's books. Along with self publishing her own books, Stacy enjoys helping aspiring authors realize their dreams. She is hoping to inspire people around the world to make a difference with her newest endeavor, nonfiction book series *Young Change Makers*. For more information and to check out Stacy's other books including her children's picture books, visit www.stacycbauer.com.

EMANUELA NTAMACK

Emanuela Ntamack is an artist and children's book illustrator, a beloved wife and mother. She is married to her Cameroonian husband Alix, and together they have two boys. She has been drawing continuously ever since she could hold a pencil. Growing up, she studied Art and Design in school and university. After she became a mother, she discovered her love for children's books illustrations. One of the biggest satisfactions of her work is when children—including her own—are inspired by the illustrations that she creates. She is thankful to God for the gift of art, and for the diversity and the beauty of Creation, which is a never-ending source of inspiration.

A **HUGE** THANK YOU TO THE FOLLOWING PEOPLE
WHO MADE A DIFFERENCE WITH THIS PROJECT

MARIANA BUSH

IN LOVING MEMORY OF
MARK SCHULTZ

IN HONOR OF
SUSAN AND MARK
CREASY

KENNEDI WASHINGTON

ALEX STEWART

THE MATTHEWS FAMILY

BRINLEY SMITH

DELANIE LOERA

MARLENE CERVANTES

MEGAN BARTEL

MARIE HOLT

ST. THOMAS
MORE SCHOOL
LYNNWOOD, WA

ERIN LONG

PENELOPE LONG

ZAEVREN TURNSTONE

JUNE HAZEUR

LOUIE BRITZ

MILES DUMLAO

MORENIKE EUBA OYENUSI

DAVID OWENS

CANDY OWENS

CARRIE SULLIVAN

NANCY SWORDS

DJ ANNIE RED

MICHELLE THORNHILL

TAYLOR

HENRY

CAMERYN

KIM JAYHAN

ROCIO GUZMAN

MS. MCGEE'S
ROOM 325

JANE WRIGHT

ASRA HAMZAVI

ABIGAIL ROSCOE

SUZANNE MULCAHY

MATINE KHALIGHI

JORDAN EVERAERT

ABIGAIL VARNER

TRAVELBETTER

INGRID MOATS

ALYSHA LANCASTER

KEN LEVINSON

ELIZABETH HILDEBRAND

TWYLIA MARION

A SPECIAL MESSAGE FROM AUTHOR STACY C. BAUER

I am so grateful to the many people who had a hand in helping to bring this series to life. I can't possibly name them all, but I wanted to mention a few. Without them, this project would not have been possible.

· The inspiring young people and their families. Thank you for allowing me to tell your stories.

· My talented illustrator Emanuela, for bringing these kids to life in a creative way.

· My wonderful friend, teacher and editor Phyllis, for being my sounding board.

· My amazing cover designer Katie, for a beautiful finish to the covers.

· My awesome designer and formatter Travis, for all of the behind-the-scenes work: attending to every detail, putting the pieces together, and so much more!

· My editors Brooke and Lor, for perfecting the text.

· My parents Nancy and Jim, for always believing in and encouraging me.

· My sisters Kori and Jessica, for being the best friends and sisters a girl could ask for.

· My husband Will, for never doubting I could do this, for making me laugh when I needed to and for forcing me to relax now and then.

· My kids Camden and Wyatt, for changing my life and giving me a reason to smile each day.

· My other family, the Bauers, for their constant support and enthusiasm for my author career.

· All of the people in my Facebook groups and my launch team and all of my amazing "author friends" (you know who you are) for your time, friendship, energy, and advice on anything and everything to do with this series.

· My Kickstarter backers for supporting my campaign and believing in me.

· And to God, for giving me the determination and energy to see this through.